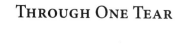

THROUGH ONE TEAR

Through One Tear **Poems**

Edward Nobles

Persea Books
New York

The author gratefully acknowledges the editors of the following magazines, where these poems first appeared: *Agni,* "Daily Dilemma"; *Boulevard,* "Toward an Open Window," "The Habit of Perfection: The First of Five"; *Carolina Quarterly,* "The God of Fish"; *Colorado Review,* "On the Head of a Pin"; *Denver Quarterly,* "After So Many Years, A First Love," "The Current Cinema," "Hearing Them," "Inside Plastic," "The Rise and Fall," "Smoking (With Duchamp)"; *Gettysburg Review,* "Nuclear Winter"; *Paris Review,* "Architectural Digest"; *Pequod,* "Loss" (Sections 1–7); *Volt,* "Through One Tear."

Acknowledgments are continued on page 87,
which constitutes an extension of the copyright page.

PERSEA BOOKS, INC.
171 Madison Avenue
New York, NY 10016

Library of Congress Cataloging-in-Publication Data

Nobles, Edward, 1954–
Through one tear : poems / Edward Nobles.
p.   cm.
ISBN 0-89255-227-1 (hardcover : alk. paper)
I. Title.
PS3564.027T48   1997
811´.54—dc21   96-50262
                              CIP

Set in Minion by Keystrokes, Lenox, Massachusetts
Printed by Haddon Craftsmen, Scranton, Pennsylvania

First Edition

for Kelly

&

for Hadley and Lydia, my daughters

CONTENTS

ONE

TWO

ONE

Solitary Union

I pull the rusted war relic
up over my body
to understand the latest unearthings
of loss and the tiny rivers of blood
that fork everywhere, further and further
out into the century, where each one
abruptly bends back, then stops.

I place my slapped ear
to the apartment's chained door,
chipped white and full of lead,
to understand the difficult life
of the hallway, and the small dirty landing
where the dark stairs beckon beseechingly
for those who must hold on, who have no choice
but to descend. Like them,

     I want to rise, but this stained blue ceiling
     is the last,
     closed above me like an iron grate.

The cold soup waits
on the kitchen counter, a thin layer
of scum surrounding a soft carrot.
History, religion, mathematics . . .
vague entities, and every light

is pulled on, the lamp shades torn off
and slashed, yet life still seeps in
around the corners, through plaster
cracks and books, until the lone
keyhole compresses
into a tiny skull, exuding
a different, dim kind of light,
a developing country
at war with itself and no one,
only the world. Turn away.

The bitter cold. The latest unearthings
of loss and the dark stairs that beckon
down.

Artillery in position, the young commander
smirks and kicks a stone determinedly
outside my window, seven stories below.
If I drop a penny, a worthless luckless penny,
with hateful precision, will it penetrate
his maroon knit cap, to exit straight through
his left boot, diagonally down

through the sad and dying earth,
and into the hands of a child, ecstatic
with his hot American discovery?
(Enormous luck
from a foreign country.)
But who will hear the body fall
on the empty street, in this mirrored night
of too many living?

Hearing waits with me
in life's
solitude.

The world's swollen dream, atomic
in its weight, painfully blooms
a dark red fire
as if it were blown apart, scattered
dislodged flowers
from a wedding bouquet
falling, slow-motion, silently,

into the arms of those who want
to love and those
that have loved but lost
what little hope is blanketed
together with the decades, beneath
stark granite and steel. One lone petal
flutters downward, then spins
solid, like a penny,

into my small sick soul.
It curls its copper heat
against my heart. At century's end.

Toward an Open Window

I have never been to Europe. Or to your house.
I did not descend the Spanish Steps. Or open
your bedroom door, climb between your sheets.
The Alps look very steep and cold, the Mediterranean
warm and blue. Not isolated

like the color of your face in this small
department store, in these plastic containers,
upon this plastic shelf. I brush you on
my hand and rub you against my cheek. I powder
my nose with your nose, my neck with your neck.

Here are your eyes—how do you create them?
Not this sad green, this melancholic
black and blue. And your lips, their swelling
ripeness. Oh, the aching, a red longing,
I love that color. I kiss you in

the little oval mirror, surrounded by thick
designer steel. Do you think she'll like this?
"Oh, yes, it's very pretty. Sir, would you like
a tissue?"—holding one toward my lips.
I wipe you off and crush you in my fist.

I have seen this witness before, her obnoxious
blue and rolling eyes, protected behind
her flimsy red counter. I won't
buy something to make her smile.
But I need you. I did not ascend

the Eiffel Tower, storm
the beach at Normandy, or collect a cupful
of concrete powder
from the Berlin Wall. Your curtains are very pretty;
I drape them over my arm as I climb in.

THE HABIT OF PERFECTION: THE FIRST OF FIVE

find the uncreated light
—GERARD MANLEY HOPKINS

I used to look into the eyes
to the soul. I felt sympathy and hurt.
Then I looked not into but
at the eyes, the size of the centers, their blackness,
the color of the outer rim,
the greens, the blues, the multiple shades of brown,
whether the whites were really white, or bloodshot
or yellowed, how the eyes opened and closed,
their amazing unconscious automation, the ability
to sleep, to stop up the light; my failings.

Of what combinations did my own eyes consist
as I took the penknife and slit? The mind
was my only mirror. But I had the sensations of touch
to reflect, the sharpness of pain, the scent of loss,
the alluring sound of my shudders and tears.
Enraptured, my soul
exited my eyes. There were angels in my ears.
I felt past the flame
to the wax. It was my next goal
to free them.

ARCHITECTURAL DIGEST

Whose woods these are I think I know . . .

I take her, painless, through the glass.
Her dress tears off. I covet that.
The glass is beautiful, sharp and steep—
the way the cracks just stop. At the table's feet.

Each wooden leg curls into a lion's paw.
Escorted by toes, in the center, a claw
that rips into the carpet, but will not tear.
I love the dress; I hold it near.

The neighbor's house, through glass, is gray.
No windows this side; they face that way.
In a magazine on the window's ledge,
where in the binding glass shards wedge,

I see a church in construction—no steeple.
Its glass, stained, looks lethal.
I want so much the dress to touch upon the glass.
I'm lost inside design, the magazine, and Mass.

Aquarium Night

Obsessed, I lurch
through the night, my head
pulled forward
by a rope. I stop
and linger
at the heels of another.
The pink lips mock
while the red lies move.
My sandy look, that sunken
beacon yellow,
sends out invitations:
the grinding surf.

Oh, Night, Aquarium Night,
you hold me captive, a wandering victim,
between your sheets of glass. This green
is the green of life. A small world,
it dims the light and hides
my longing. Oh, Heart, you too
are led here by a rope. (The fog
horns bark and the sea
winds blow.) The walls are thin
and you don't know it.
The water lies stagnant
and the moon grows dim:
last bubble. Be in love and
watch it rise, together with her,
beyond this night
and into the arms of another.

THROUGH THE DESERT

The drive moved me. Alone, I thought, and yet
not alone. The seeds, tradition's roots, pushed vine
upward out my eyes and up around the skull. I wore a crown.
The landscape reshaped itself. This conflict with the mind,
a wrestling with vision, wore me down and I
stopped the car, locked the wheel, and leaned back against the seat.
I knew when I had entered, in March, the first day of Spring,
that thirty-three would be the year, an itching
in the heart, an aching in each palm, the drastic year of Christ.
But where could this experience lead? What could be gained
in another's heaven?   I started back up the car.
My thirty-three years of self led me, I knew not where but
quite well what lay ahead: the fight. The landscape flexed,
rippled muscle outward in great heat, tradition's taunt. But I would not
stop, and drove straight past, over the limit. A fine line means so much.

Inside Plastic

The hairdryer against my forehead burns.
Some plants have little hearts
and if you fill the heart with water
it can hold the fluid for a long, long time.
I tried it once, and the inside core, it rotted.
My fists are like this; the skin turns shriveled and pink.
I slowly flower open my hands and lift up
the palms, cup them deep inside the sockets.

The department store is closing.
I stare through purple curtains into a stockroom.
Small yellow boxes line the wall.
My mother takes me by the hand, some thirty years ago,
and tells me the boxes each hold something special,
but we will have to wait
until next time, *we will see next time,* tugging now
across the grave, *we have to go.*

My hand inside a plastic bag
does not die, the way a small child would,
though the fingers snap frantic against it,
the palm sweats and everything stops.
I place the hand inside a corrugated box,
a small thick box, noted for its strength,
"up to a hundred pounds,"
but something is not right.

A Hat Upon the City

We ascend, together, the tower.
You in night blue; I dressed in this night.
No hats or open umbrellas.
It's the only time we didn't say
we had to go. We move on.

The wind howls, swirling its fists,
wrapping the rising skyscrapers.
Guilt hangs from the wires,
fifty-two stories high.
Visions of torture; tears
of betrayal and hate. We land
on the wrong floor, a room
full of gazers, staring out across the city.
No one takes their face from the glass.

We rise again, this time on mechanical wings.
A witch's brew, the minutes foretell
meanings of many levels. We push on,
building to building. Millions
of rectangles, sheets of thick glass.
Everyone holds a light
behind darkness, whether that power is on
or off. This is the only way
we can make it—with this knowledge—
as the roar engulfs us
and we fall

moonward, into one another's face.
An open window. And a hat
drops upon the city.
It leaves us, not quite together,
in daylight. It is a place
where no one belongs.

Nuclear Winter

When the sky fell, the earth turned blue.
The trees, the tenements, the cars and buses
soaked up the sky and changed from outside in, in color,
to blue. The children ran frantically in adult directions. My wife,
dressed fashionably in blue, took my hand and, with sadness
in her deep blue eyes, led me behind the house, down the long incline, and into
the woods. We waded in blue snow through blue trees.
An iridescent crow, blue, flew from a branch, and a fox
lay in our tracks, oblivious to our passing. He licked his blue fur
with melancholic eyes. The years pass very quickly with this earth.
In that time, we had two children, the son and daughter
we always dreamt of, and they knelt above us, like two granite stones,
ghostly figures praying, for the love of God, for what we had become:
a family moved by that one clear color, blue, beneath the blue snow.

No Hope When

Tongue so coarse,
a lion's lick
can draw blood
with a single stroke.

There is no hope when
the power is so total,
so overwhelming
and oppressive.

Only awe
as the drawn blood beads.

Through One Tear

I had a dream.
And in that dream I dreamt that I was dreaming.
And in my dream I was dreaming
that I lay on a pillow sleeping,
not too soundly, which led me to have
a vivid dream. And in this dream I dreamt
that I had the covers on and I was warm
beneath the covers between the sheets.

And in this bed I dreamt that I was sleeping soundly
until the alarm went off (in that dream)
which I slapped off and fell back asleep,
into another dream. This dream was very strange.
It was a dream of multiple dreams, and each dream
was divided into a nation, and each nation
was a part of a continent, which was part of the planet,
in a universe of untold dimension.
But nothing was real; it was all a dream.

Some of the dreams began breaking up
like torn photographs of lovers dispersing on a lake.
And dreams began infringing on each other, like years,
until I did not know whether I was really awake
or awake in a dream. Then I dreamt it was a new century.
And then I really woke and staggered to the window.
Outside the window were people sleeping.
But they floated on a lake, dreaming.

The wet dead leaves looked like buildings in a dead city.
Their tiny tears blinked like desperate windows.
I looked through one tear and shivered.
I saw there the vacant streets, the broken vows,
the stark assembly of blackened steel. The moon-
rippled moon—disturbing—moving along so many ceilings,
ceilings almost white. And I watched dreams burning
like pieces of torn love (the wind painfully silent), whirling on the black lake
toward the center of the earth, its damaged inner ear.

Two

WAREHOUSE

1.

The strain and collapse
of a large
wooden crate.

The closed, perfectly spaced,
metal painted door.

Ten boxes
to a pallet, ten dozen
pallets, or more, and the never-ending

concrete

taking in, drawing out,
soaking up

time.

2.

No barking, baying, I
slide between the bottom
of a box and the top
of another. Flat,
slightly moist, mildewing,
brown. I take

a deep breath,
sigh of relief,
pull my limbs in.

3.
Packaged
machinery.
A slight
clink
of metal
if I move.

4.
The penetrating
horizontal line
pressing against my spinal

rings where the two flaps
of the upper box come together

but do not touch.

5.
The corrugated rub
where the water
thinned the paper
and the box's ribs

wore through. Wet
box smell, beautiful
box world.

      6.
My nostrils flare
and a few thoughts
fold into their own
boxes, thin rectangles

enclosing space. I climb
inside each one
alone
for a moment

to be free.

The Non-Naturals: There are Seven

Why the most natural actions of a man's life
should be called his Non-naturals is another question.
—Laurence Sterne

I was sleeping, when the food—
lamb and wine—was set before me.
I took a bite of air and moved
my eyes about the room.
They rested on a plate.
The affectations of the mind.
To excrete or retain. To breath
or eat meat. These are not essential
to animal life or health. By accident or abuse,
the unnaturals bring pain, luscious,
extenuating pain—that sorrow.
I opened the book and I
closed the book. I was impressed
to push the list to eight. To desire.
But this, as all else,
is another question, and one on which
we should not rest. The ship moves
against the sea. And the men,
those bleak anomalies, move within the ship.

THE CURRENT CINEMA

1.
I did not want
to die and so
I defended
the current cinema.

2.
I alone
counted
ten rows down and
five seats in.

3.
I sat beside
a gentle seat
with synthetic
fabric torn.

4.
A single wire,
sprung, pushed
upward
from the center

5.
for all the world
to see. For all
the world
to see.

6.
I alone, it seemed
(*seem* a subtle
word), pressed
the wire's point.

7.
There could have been
a perfect
circle, or a
square, a perfect

8.
square,
but there was not.
No blood. A rectangle
is not a house, is not

9.
a home. Without
the lights, I still
could see. The popcorn lost
was a mystery.

Nostalgia for the Road to Salvation

1.

A rusted screw, threads stripped
and Phillip's head
near-perfect cross
mashed from some past frustration.
I place its blunted point
carefully to the basement's dark wall
and, pushing with all my weight,
crucify it more.

2.

Ancient circular power saw blade,
aged beyond use, and yet
its carbide tips are sharp enough
that if you fling it
with force, like a Frisbee,
flipping the wrist,
it still has the power
to do damage. See.

3.

All I need now
is this hammer, with its broken
claw and battered head
which I bang against my thumb
because it is too young
and perfect. It needs to remember.
Remember this:

The Rise and Fall

We could not find from where
the breakage took place
in the nearby forest. The branches
fell, this was certain, and the father,
with his blonde beard and gold-
plated glasses, opened, suddenly,
one of those strollers
that fold up

so completely, you think of the invention
of the umbrella
or of society, its developments,
Japan and the Computer Age.
Perhaps someone has gone back a few centuries
and is felling the decades with an axe.
It must be a well-thrown axe,
the speed with which the branches fall.

The Hieratic Head of Pound

Tching prayed on the mountain and
wrote MAKE IT NEW
on his bathtub
Day by day make it new
cut underbrush,
pile the logs
keep it growing.
—Ezra Pound

The Hieratic Head of Pound, the
personal withdrawn into a force,
the force unshakable, the unshakable
foreseen, yet only by that force.
Only when in action did it count.
The creator, a mere twenty-three,
dead. The subject, protruding,
an axe through a wall.
The antithetical there, inside:

Ah, Mr. Pound, welcome.
Ah, Doctor, step outside
for a moment, into the wind!
But, Mr. Pound, I am in the wind,
as is my wife, the artist, and all
our friends: Dr., Dr., and Dr.
The elements lash from within the axe.
The onlookers wade from one quest
to another. Do you know
what Hemingway said about the bull?
"No." You have learned his lesson
well: brevity. Each man carries

an axe dug deep inside himself,
with pleasure. Their blades are very
slight. Small, yes, but can one
see them? These subtle warriors
laugh in circles, bloodied
with liquor, around their host: chop, chop.

CLASSROOM

How to make a moment matter? Tears, toil, darkness
can't do it. Nor tradition. Nor lines around
the eyes and mouth. The forced pressure to raise a hand,
a plump white hand, as if the hand once held
aloft would mean a victory. But this is all and must be
out of necessity, when we are truly ourselves, truly living—
when is that? The feel of a breast
pushed tightly against the wall,
the nipple aroused by the cold plaster, the thighs pushed open
by the knee, the cry of entry. But wasn't
the subject French? And isn't the topic
the fashions of spring? Or it will be spring
once winter has departed, an army in defeat,
and the cry of a bell startles to push on.
Too late now to raise a hand. You are stuck
with this: the victory of an axe
as it falls by the synchronized force
of muscle and weight
down into the schooled seat
of the imagination.

A Way of Life

My mind. Would not. Start.
For lack. Of movement. My body,
draped over the chair, only sank further
as I tried to stand. Or: memory thought
I had tried to stand, but I had no thought and no
recollection: a series of negatives, fully out-blown
and healthy, a body in the womb of this room
where a light burned, illuminating the books and
the corners of the bookcase. Somewhere: music, actors,
education. Can I learn though locked inside?

I read a book and wondered on its meaning.
I read a book, but me, myself, I
had already drifted a few years
into the past, down into its music,
a different kind of wave, a turnip.

Is this the struggle I will have to report?
What will the children remember?
Is heritage the honing or the rusting of the blade?
Worth the tale if lacking thrust or strike?
Are blood and fallen bodies our only hope?

When the telephone rang, my mind turned
toward it. My hand reached, striking for its sound.
The sound was my miracle, and I the new-to-sight.
But I did not lift the receiver; I held it there

with all my weight, feeling the power rising, the desperate
caller, and the painful pounding
of birth, of breath, of life.
I held it there beyond its silence, held it until my left eye
twitched, and my lips opened only once
before they closed. And one day passed into another.

DAILY DILEMMA

I accept the plate before me now
and request only, but request only,
to eat
without scrunching up, as I do,
my face
in total disgust (revulsion), anger, pain.
I wish to eat
their shit calmly, unswervingly,
even outwardly pleased
until I alone have won
what it is I can't remember
and then can turn to the dark
of the basement later
to spit it out in triumph, laughing.

Yet I grimace, weakly
savoring in the no-reward
I receive, the immediate gratification
of showing them outright, a mere several feet
from their faces, most disrespectfully,
that I will eat
their shit, because I will go that far
(because I have to; I know not why),
but I do not like it, won't
like it, will never like it.

They give me more, continually

fill my plate, to feed my grimace.
Not the choices I would have selected.
But I choose now
to center my anger
into the spoon, pressurizing
the metal handle with my fingers
into some precious symbol,

symbol of my self, that is my anger,
and in solemn, perfect steadiness,
hold the spoon, filled to the rim with their own
shit, in their own faces,
saying, swearing, "Here, you take it"
to myself, stop, break, laugh,
push it back
into my scrunched-up face
and eat it, contemplating freedom.

Smoking (With Duchamp)

My niece is cold because, well, because
my knee is cold. The nearness
is clothed in darkness, which is not the darkness
of poets, but merely a lamp
shut off by the little white
knob, which you turn clockwise on
or off, or counterclockwise and you hold
the knob in your hand. Beautiful hands.
Her name is beautiful, too. Framed
the evening brings with it light, but no
sentiment, no stars and no moon
to be seen. No one is looking.
I hang out the window
my pipe from my lips. Within each
puff is my thoughts. The one
that just passed said, "Those buttocks are _____."
But, then, thoughts are private
as one parts with them only when urged
from some inner solid weight.
I can't restrain. I've expressed myself
with beautiful hands too long. Nothing
but summer heat to distract us.
And the no stars and the no moon.

New Moon

and when, though the earth rotates on the same
invisible axis, the seasons have been displaced—

•

As I thought, a black ball appeared
to mark the spot between
thoughts' transitions. On close
inspection (as I was still

thinking; I could not stop), the ball
appeared to be not "ball"
but several balls, innumerable balls,
as each ball that marked a spot

was different, with slight
variations in color, or shape, or placement
in the hairline place between a thought
transition. The juxtaposition

of thought to ball
altered the ball or thought
in dependence on one's concentration.
As these were my thoughts and demarcations,

others could not share
in the subtleties, the marked dramatics
of this static (because inner) show.
My mind alit, circling with questions,

inspirations, revelations
of which only I

could answer, pursue, perish in
or be awakened. Beneath each circle, what light?

●

One thought, one ball appeared.
It shimmered seductively
in the center of my mind. I followed
and arriving at this destination
I stood before it. I reached
my arms around it, held its black rims.
A halo; a fragile plate.
It began to roll and I, captured in its beauty,
began to walk
around the lake, circling between two thoughts,
one of the planets,
the other of empty space.
I was nothing but humbled, a head,
swollen in thought, beneath a hat (brown).

●

Till human voices wake us and we drown.

AFTER SO MANY YEARS, A FIRST LOVE

(On First Looking into Robert Hughes'
THE SHOCK OF THE NEW)

Going through photos in a book.
Paintings by Picasso, Duchamp, Monet.
Commenting. Me: I like this one.
You: No, this one is much better.
And the photo of a painting
by the German, George Grosz,
holds you captive, and I acknowledge
the bizarreness of the ugliness: the suspended dark hand.

A saucer, cup and spoon
(page 243)
a *Luncheon With Fur,* domestic
ideas softened by death. You laugh
and say, how nice, you should hang
that on your wall.

A small series of photos,
diminutively entitled, *The Doll.*
In each of the ten is a girl
exposed, pink splotched and
contorted in various stages
of impossible redress. In one
she's all leg and huge mound.
In another, the big bubbles of breasts
swallow the head whole—a blond
Lilith, smiling, going down.

The *Seated Bather*
is nude, too, with stone for
thighs and a mouth approaching
stiff claws. We could feel for hours
in a kiss. And here we have
Magritte's *Human Condition,*
number one.

POPULAR MECHANICS

I pull her panties to the floor
    and hold them there
against the floorboards. The measured
    lines widen and
close, though all along to the wall
    each is exact-
ly two inches from the other;
    the carpenter
saw to that. In the distance, small

    clouds of dust
accumulate beneath the bed; they
    glide along, slowly pushed
by an invisible gust, until they
hesitate at an iron leg. The cloth
    is blue—I remember
    it—white cotton on the inner pouch.
    The chair legs

    catch the light
from the window and hold it. In one
    I can see the entire
circumference of the sun. A red-yellow
marble rolls through the dust and stops at
    a penny. The elastic
    band contorts and expands. The cloth is
    soft. Under

          the dresser,
        the bent corners of a magazine.
            Popular Mechanics?
Probably, with colored photos. The floor-
boards are greyed, cold. It is still winter. The
          hot cloth plays dead. I look
        up at the sky outside the window.
            The small clouds

of dust accumulate beneath
        the bed. I hold
tight, then begin to slide—slowly,
        not moving, up-
ward, outward, into space. I hes-
        itate a few
years at an iron leg, then move
        on, wondering
at the blackness, the exactness
        of the measured line.

Three

Loss

1.

When I awake some day, past evening,
and the child cries, her spirit broken,
having found a shard with the smudged
drawing of a hoof. Where did she learn
such feeling? There is a blessedness
in the breeze. In Lapland, the Lapp
herd the reindeer throughout the season.
The heart stopped, the horns torn out, meat
cut into its various sections, the process ends.

2.

For some, a joke; with its massive
clumsy body, bizarre beak, and ugly
little wings
of no use for flight. Three or four

were enough to feed
a hundred men. The persevering mind
endowed the dodo stature
and eternal life. We pray
for its survival.

And traveling saints,
well-mounted on a switch,
ride journeys through

the infected air, like a Lapland witch.

Where did she, or even I,
learn such faith
and unsettling hope? We long
for the relief
of her betrayal.

3.

Everything was going down,
dying, sinking in mud. I watched
my family's lives fade, change. I watched
the amoeba divide, eat, be eaten
in that constant flux
of white scum. Something transformed
behind the eyes, panicked and pushed,
desperate. The sockets ached, the world
pushed through, and life
exploded.

LePore of Braintree,
age 55, suddenly, on Feb. 20, Grace A.
Retired Lowell seamstress. Beloved wife of Francis W.
Devoted mother of Paul T. Memorial Services
thru Tuesday at. Remembrances may be made to.

He attended the Church of the Most Precious Blood,
in Hanover, all his life. Yet now, at death,
his mother insists he cannot be buried
with the blessings of the church.

She wants him burned, for burning
her life into hell. She won't even attend
the service or the train. Everything

was going down, dying. I watched. I waited.
I joined the procession; the blaring of horns;
the small band; the strangers following behind.
Listen and rejoice! Take up the hammer and pound!
for all we've lost, the precious Lord hath found!

4.

His hands are bleeding. Elongated splinters
capture the light. It's beautiful.
Would you make me one? Not on a string.
I want one that will really fly.
Battle-weary,
they waited for jeeps to evacuate the dead.
I want you to know
that your letter really meant something.
Not just in terms of being romantic,
but of how I see myself. And you.

The waters came
and many were missing. It was strange
canoeing through windows, pulling out bodies
from beneath plumbing and beds. Not all the bodies
surfaced, or were counted as missing
when they did. I almost cut my arm
on a piece of glass. I thought about it,
and you, all winter.

5.

The headlines are encapsuled, boring, and the "Arts
and Books" section is alluring for its brevity.
The business
of America is sports. A sucking sound.
She pulls her sexy red head into rubber,
her feet into rubber, and splashes away. The sound

of rubber. The flowers die; the pine and oak
climb down; the landscape progresses
from old to new. Some gain their wings
in the greening depths. But if we really are

blank black slates
onto which our lives are drawn,
someone has been dragging,
haphazardly, an eraser
hard across my wordy life

changing	FORTUNE	
to	FORT	
and	BLOSSOM AT ALL COST	
to just	LOS	T

6.

Surrounded by decay, sensation's skeleton,
I slide my broken hand (numb with feeling)
gently along my lover's skin, her spirit charged
with a radiant energy. I pull on my shiny
new boots, made in America, manmade,
back the tractor into a stall, feed the one or two heifer,

and collapse the barn, forever.
A beautiful black asphalt, black rainbow,
cascades endlessly
across the plain. Around the globe,

we were each involved in a private search
for the whitened Arctic regions,
the magic circle. But I found
only the shoreline in Maine, where we vacationed,
and Boston, where we lived (and died) in hope and fear
enough to last, unpleasant to the married ear. This desolate
joking was a way to accept. What? We had
to do something. Light brown
in summer, white-gray in winter,
capable of traveling

up to forty miles a day,
dragging twice its own weight, the reindeer
has grown mythic, its heartbeat godlike
in its mute tug
against time. I saw then

the white ring. Had I known its location
all along? But I was only
pretending. This lost love, spinning.
The skull. The worldly. Such special places.

7.
Through the precious moments, a sliver
of light, I can see the field. One oak

to the right; then the boot to the head. I lay there,
face down against the damp boards
for hours, what appeared
to be windows, seeing the field,
climbing the branches, the thick bark with its
invisible movement—so alive! and the spring
there below breathing deeply, ecstatically.

I waved my torn shirt
down at the people and shouted.
They came up the path, marching in file.
No one was laughing. But then
one child, a girl of about ten, she . . . I watched for this

through wind and wail. The tide turned up,
as I drew my breath, and poured straight in
its broken speech. The sound of hooves
against crushed stone. The antlers, of various dimensions,

thrown down into the bed
of the truck. The banging green metal. And miles away, the gulls
skirt the rocks, afraid to land; and the skate
tuck their bellies
to the bottom of the sea. Took her hand

and just pointed. A deer
on a plate of glass. Every part
of the creature painted
in reverse, a hundred years ago, the direct
opposite to the mirror, above which
the painting rests. The salt taste
touched my lips.

8.

The initial conception was more
realistic, more tragic, with you
and me together in the heavens, while the world
roared all around us. But in the end
we were outside
in the midst of that roar. And the heavenly,
the mute, were removed from the vibration of air, no sound.
They lived through the eyes
and listened. I stopped the car

about a block from her house—betrayed?—waited
an hour, got out, and continued on foot.
Around the fountain, the white spray
dampened my clothes. A crash
of hooves in the underbrush. The massive
furred chest. The antlers searching, feeling,
the brutality of air. The deep affliction
mirrored in her eyes. The eyes
mirrored in the world all around us. We depend so dearly
on the dimness and the cloth. What could make that touch
of darkness go away? The antlers fall and everyone
listens. There is a difference in the sea.

9.

At each corner, I made a tower. The stones
possessed a power all their own. And the words
collected in a similar fashion. But this
was not all. There were many
adjustments to be made. First, the juxtapositions

needed to be perfect, and the joints
tight; if not, chinked. As a stranger,
I held you in my arms
a thousand years, and swore then and there
that I would never

leave you.
He is learning
(solemnly to self)
well behind his desperate eyes
(as if to soul)
the epistemology
of loss (counting
the many ways

to make it
to the water). The ball rolls
across the years, and the child.
But then
it disappears. Which,
the ball or child? By heavens
if you could have but changed hearts
with some bloody Lapland witch! The silo full, the mountains
growing old, tree line diminishing, the explorers
pushed further and further into the distance.
And the bridge.

I walked across a tightrope all my life.
But this was not all. There were many,
many, and each one held a candle. We moved
outward toward the light, and the branches

welcomed the sun. *Listen*
and rejoice! I shouted, waving
my shirt; the salt taste touched my lips.
It tasted for all the world just like.
Like what? The sand? The sea?
No, not like them there tastes. Then what?
It was like, well, like a. Like what?
Like blood.

10.

The faces pushed against wire fences.
The eyes open with longing toward the open field.
We remove the fencing, but the faces remain.
Pushed now against the field. We scatter
the seed into the long ditches. They run from one end
to the other. We bury the seed
and wait for the faces.

11.

Scrutinize, scrunch down, lay low to the earth
and listen. A shrill power runs through the wires.
Missiles churn the loam, create beautiful shrapnel.
Picasso or Braque? At this point it's difficult to tell.

The carpenters soak the wood for hours, then fold it
into boxes, caress them oval and smooth.
In one, our family papers—birth and marriage certificates,
the photos, clippings—all brown, barely readable,
but treasured. I take the box into the field

and fold the loam over the wood. The leaves unroll
over and over, over the years. The faces
on the family tree. They took the women
and children, the old men. We heard the departing of jeeps.

12.

We follow the tracks to the stream, cross the stream,
and continue across the field
to the woods. A movement of leaves.
Rifles raised, no warning, we fire.
The echoing chunks of wood. The fifties look,

with blond furniture and a fireplace.
The perfect family in their perfect house,
exactly like the neighbors. She was so happy.
Or so we thought. It must be difficult
to lose one's footing. We looked everywhere, even in the . . .

14.

We gather dried sticks and, later,
berries and fruit. Soon the jeeps arrive
and the shouting faces. A pull of the scarf,
the burning torture of lights. Then
it was back to the fences. In Lapland, the Lap—

What? A broken record. The yard was tiny,
but we decided we had to build something.
You suggested a wall. The seagulls looked
dirty. And you walked around the house
measuring our losses. There wasn't even reason to mention . . .

15.
Three miles from this place, in a wood,
I mark a twig the Spring
bird dropped, stopped,
suspended in the air.
The light thing
           trembled downward
                       in a graph, then lost
                       itself
           among the leaves.
The last leaves fall; the snow and wind
beat against the bark. All will be lost.

16.
We placed mimeographed notices
in every window. Promised a reward.
It wasn't much but it pleased your mother.
It took me about a week to collect all the stones.
I tried many designs, but few came close
to what was needed. The wall had to be both
traditional and contemporary, completely
new, an understandably difficult task
when dealing with such an element,
one that has been here so long, so long
set in its ways. And isn't it amusing

how the Lapp use them like dogs
or mules? Huge deer dragging children around in carts.
Your parents were married much longer than us.
I've always admired those

who work with the land. How could you just bury something
that can't die? I wouldn't want it buried
in my town, or even in my state. I'd be afraid
to drink. Afraid of the radiation.

17.

Last year's vacation was exciting, but your father wouldn't go.
We saw the Alps and the spirit of St. Francis. Our first trip
and now we reminisce. You retire early and work
diligently around the house. The high heels stand
empty, upright, on the porch. A grazing buck
knocks one over. Loss is an obsession, a song.
I really like your shoes. Especially the heels.
I want a belt made from an eagle or an egret or a deer.
I want my whole body covered with exotic
furs. I want. Over there, somewhere in the west.

I don't want to be unhappy, or happy
in the wrong way. They wear those coats; in fact,
utilize every part. Not many can wear the fabric of their work.
A machinist covered with grease; a clock with a broken
arm. Even in the basement, with all its
memories. I am sorry for the things that I've done.

18.

I am sorry for the things that I've done.
He washes his hands several times that evening
and listens at the living room door for her confession.
Everyone is laughing; no tragedy breaks in.

Except this one, as he turns again
to wash his hands.

He knew it was a sin, knew it was his aunt,
and therefore wrong, but something beyond,
deep within himself, reached out
and gently pushed his hand
against her breast.
He could even feel the plump bud
of her nipple through the blouse.

The chase at hem, and horns blow
at reindeer and the dreadful roe.

That moment! What height to which he was flung!
But the reproof rushed through his ears
and knocked him to himself; the room rose
and he was drowning. That night, she wishes
him pleasant dreams, nighty-night for sleep,
as if nothing had happened. He longs for the relief
of her betrayal. With these are mingled

the bones of red deer and roe, but the reindeer
has not yet been found. How many times can one
avert ones eyes? How many weeks? Months?
He presses his hand against the pillow
but cannot sleep. The country is quite rocky,
covered with a white moss and sparse tufts
of weed upon which the reindeer eat.

19.

In the middle of the forest, the sensitive brutal man
lay down in the burnt-out mud, beside his murdered lover's bones,
curled up and threw in his shadow, the inverse of rage,
lunged slowly inward to die. There on the precipice
the solitary deer

swayed its large antlers, bucking, kicking up dust
for something that would never come. Absence
has brought us nothing, so we can't complain.
In the past, men drove them here on purpose,

to force them over. Afterward they would
gather down below and have great feasts
in the mud, among the bones. The blood
was their rejoicing. And still the darkness came.

20.

My throat swells up. She's not to be found.
A belt around the bars. I'm not afraid, but.
They tore down the local shopping mall
and planted a forest. The whole town was eventually

razed to provide room for more trees. And God
came down and handed us each a candle.
I transformed mine into my sweaty palms,
made a pair of dice. The priest swung the bell
and preached. They carved their names into the pew.

Patty loves Jimmy. But what priest wouldn't

annul such a marriage? No one returned the papers,
fulfilled the proper requirement. No one offered me bread
or a piece of candy. No one would even bet.
She was so lonely. Snake eyes.
A nuclear freeze. An erection.

Even the priest was impressed. Keep it from the children.
"Dad?" Lock the door and pretend we're sleeping.
"Mom?" The sand blows across the bodies,
transforms the flames. Name the children
after presidents. A romance of the sea. The little island.

                    21.
I sat upon the shore, a small town in Maine,
fishing for lesser gods, with the arid
plain behind me. Shall I at least
set my verse in order? Nothing could be more
in line with what we wanted, the way a mason
sets his strings across
a fifty foot expanse
to keep the stone straight,
moving up and down
his level as the wall becomes
concrete, the blueprints

discarded, a map of an ancient city
that never could be found. Unlike the antlers
in their crude majesty, the eyes exude
an innocence, a portrait
of rugged sadness. Nothing should be so

romantic, so remarkably elegant
as this, a weakness over years.
I drew in my line and capped it on my own:
a wall against the ruins. And even there
in the attic, she was nowhere to be found.

22.

Could she have drowned? The river is
practically in the backyard, and the island
is really tiny. Nuke 'em all. The antlers
protrude from above the bed. The reindeer hooves
pound on the rug, ripping the fabric. I turned
the key, but I couldn't get inside. Plug in the electric.
The season's done, sensation's gone. Wash your.

They filled the large bay with pilings,
stone and concrete. This was very successful
in pushing the waste away from the pier.
They tore down the pier and the buildings and
later constructed our apartment. The waste

drew nearer, staining the windows.
The rents are very expensive in Boston.
Look at these two porcelain seagulls, wings outspread,
dropping from a thread in the storefront window.
They don't even try to make them realistic any more.
Remember the past? No. The heart stopped,
the horns torn out. We can do it here, but no noise.

23.

Remember how the movie ended with a kiss,
fine-lined lips, swelled red
and rolled seductively around
a spot of black? Let the stars
imitate that; and the planets.
We can do it here, at the Stock Exchange
or in the subway, but no talking.
Be discrete. They herd them
day in, day out. A way of life.

24.

I wanted him so badly
that I crushed into his face.
He stiffened and clumsily
tried to back away and talk.
But then I made him part
his lips, drew his hands
inside my blouse. I baby-sat
every chance I could.
And when he had me
to that point, my body aching,

I made him stop. I knew then
that I didn't want to have a child,
not before I'd even reached fifteen.
We broke up that summer,
and by next fall, I . . . Earthly losses

are remedies for covetousness. The small angel
hovered over his shoulder, not indifferent

to the beauty of her needs. Love, that excuses
no one loved from loving,
seized me so strongly with delight in him
that, as you see, he never leaves my side.

                    25.
We are all told how real it is,
shown grayed illustrations. Remember
that November? the wake? the shiny odd box?
And I
bow down, broken, but alive. The stars
on my face are childhood scars
and the ache in my eyes
is only the glasses. One pair too weak; the other
too heavy. And naked, I'm blind. She wouldn't

have gone into the forest. The remains
point to an organism similar in some aspects
to birds; in others, to mammals.
Came home but the home was gone.
A beautiful waterfall fell beautifully
through the middle of a mall. But I
had shopping to do, so I couldn't wait.

I wanted to be near you, be for you
something special, a gift you would cherish
all your life. The most effective agent
is the pressure of the species. Of all the animals
of the deer kind, the reindeer
is the most extraordinary, the most useful.

26.

Pitched toward the last
love, the lost
hope, *the last*
dream, the lost
song, the last
loss, the.

27.

Imagine a child's clumsy drawing
of a deer on a plate of glass, a mirror framed
in elaborate gold leaf, an antique,
and the father in a rage,
but they offer him three million dollars to break the mirror
and never mention it to the child. No,
not now, no deer, nothing. Tell the child nothing.
Mirrors echo for some, not all. Tupperware,

bandaids, bonded teeth, the ozone layer
practically gone. Slate wiped clean. Three years
before the dentures and then the crystal clear.
Get me a knife, someone, will you, quick!
Tell the child nothing. And in the romantic
Black Forest. And somewhere, also, in the South.

Four

PRAYER FOR THAW

Ancient rites of Spring
[The brain swells inside the skull.
The fluids bubble from out of the belly.
The sulfurous odor, odor of the heart,
lifts from off the chest and in and out
of nose and mouth. The skin shrinks
along the legs and tightens on the pelvis.
The penis bent, a dusty slug; and the anus reeks
a hollow dark. One sliver of a nerve
slides along a crack, around the rim,
the labyrinth of night, to the outer ear:
a slow trickle. The gutters full of ice.]
work your spell on me!

To America's Shore

A priest in the window. A street
with granite curbing lying on its side, uprooted
and washed ashore. Sidewalks
beautifully buckled from heavy frost. Street lamps,
their cries of safety stopped, muffled in fog; they drop
their knives in scattered pools. Fissures in cool asphalt.

The late night passively takes this desire
that rises toward no one; helmeted, defiant,
pointing upward against the glass. The hour turns
and clicks off the only light. To what passion
is the soldier victim, the nation collapsing
upon itself in the dying century?

Determined, I walk these streets, my boot-
scuffs echoing like machinery, distant weaponry.
Reluctant voyeur, I am startled, repulsed
by my reflection: Homo sapien in broken glass.
I whip the wind-rippled puddles with a broken stick.

The racing clouds uncloud the moon and crimson
skies reveal their magic. Oh, God of Night,
spring storms that claim and then reveal,
I revel in the mystery of my soul's passions,
your dark mirrors glimmering with embers of torn red.
Everything is hopeless, useless, desperate. And yet,
I crave. For what? Saplings glisten.

Killed two birds with one stone.
We're nothing now; both alone.
Broken branches, broken bones.
Black birds cross the telephone.

Black windows work black filament.
Membranes painfully reveal the night.
A woman stands there, each palm housed
in a cold pane, fingers outstretched against the wood.
She pours longing down the boulevard.

Red light falls into puddles, burns on each blade of grass.
And in the hunter-green flower boxes lie the tubers.
And in the gutter lies the book, its pages buckled
from a burst of rain. And the black glistening streets all weave
together, with houses, wires and windows,
down toward the sea.

LOST IN ART WEATHER (Far From Arles)

—VINCENT VAN GOGH 1853–1890

I *love* him,
we would say when we were young.

Drive carefully,
I told her. But she would not listen.

The snow had turned the roads to fields; one long
narrow field outside my window where

no ravens flew, with no
black hatch marks. Or blue ones.

Or yellow.
He was dead at thirty-seven.

The field went on and on—to where?
Onto his knees. A life for several million.

Thank God he had a brother. And I, a sister,
lost in the insanity of this weather.

The God of Fish

I have known the sad eternity of the cod heaven
—Robert Bly

1) One, and one, and another
one: I watch the bubbles rush
their monotonous advance. Some
cling to the surface floor
before they expire in that pathetic
poof. Silent their fall, but audible,
barely tinctured, to the great
membrane (they know no sense),
the god of fish. Steam filters

through, coursing in schools
within the brain, mingles with the cigar's
grey smoke, collects about the ears,
the bunched curtains, and my mouth's
out-pursed prayer for hope. Here,
in this cancerous shroud,
I can think, and lose myself
in this one vacuum thought. Here,
I can know no thing and be
pure longing, a fish, its thrashing stopped,
for it is dead. Or I will be

transformed, a god of fish,
and each shall before me lie
outstretched on a golden plate,
surrounded by sprigs of plastic
(perfect through time) and a slice

of lemon, for its bitterness.
And I, shrouded in adoration,
shall appoint their fate.

2)   Yes and no, a flickering:
the electric sting. Yes and
no, the undulation, the filament,
the slimeful ascension
toward the sun. The iron plates,
the filagree, tail and fin.
Greens, golds, blues,
black, opaque and red.

3)   Oh to be of this world
in heaven and not
have to be this one
sense, which won't submerge,
this woman,
who courses through the never-ending
corals of my brain, no fish in any sea,
who knows me for what I am,
no god of anything,
but my own longing.

METAMORPHIC

I no longer know what I look like.
I haven't seen a face in years.
Do not look in a lover's eyes. At my age
a window is a hostile thing.

Eyeglasses in the bedside table,
lost in dust, beneath dead petals;
lenses cracked, black arms broken,
watching, watching. Wait for me.

Somewhere someone else is dying.
Death gods stitch the unholy shroud.
The surviving mother's mind is missing,
her aspiring neck wrung in grief.

A cockroach split
frees the worm. Fetus of a soul.
Mirrors, eyes, windows, glass.
I am tired. Dream for me.

More than centuries, so it
seems, and I lean against
the swollen cheek
below the eye. The dehydrated bone
cracks, and my hand, surprised,
falls through
up to the knuckles in skull. A relief

of dust
rises from the face when something
starts, recoils in fear. But something else
is satisfied
with this collapse, obscene assault. It rolls
my fingers into a fist. Not intrusion, but
replacement, a welcoming in.

Then I turn
from the mirror, from my desk
tired of myself
and the repetition of my feelings.
My feelings. I watch the dust
dry the blood. It flakes from my hand like clay
from the sculptor's chisel. Effacing

or becoming? The aching sockets
make a narrow entrance,
an even smaller

source of my escape. In vengeance,
I plug each socket with an eye.
Bloodshot, an alcoholic flicker
sparks along the brain. Becoming

or effacing? Stumbling, I drop
the skull and kick
the alchemic debris, oh sacred hand!
across the room. It glows
there in the dust, disengaged
but ready
to make my peace. Behind my ear: a pen.

The Whole World

There are hands
that know me.

And hands
that do not know me.

Though they
touch me.

On the Head of a Pin

Through the thin
    needle
of an eye,
    you can prick
the darkness
    to discover
blood, and
    eventually,
the splinter
    that cripples
your heart.

The full moments
    sink, the oldest
collapse, the skies
    fall down,
Christian Little.

    Faith
so small, it fits
    in the pocket,
in a tulip, in the
    hole
of an ear. Hearing
    shut down, sight
invisible
    and the mouth

stopped up
  with no light.

  The ghosts
are not. Holy ghosts.
  Not tears.
Dancing and
  darkness and . . .

The soul
  is something. Must be
something. At least
  a dream
in a small, thin
  box. You cannot
see, but feel
  its buzz
die when you
  block
your heart's ear.

Discover
  something. Discover
this: How can we
  trick you
into your self,

  dear life?

THORN OF LIGHT

1.

If there is nothing
you can save us from,
then save us from ourselves.
(We are nothing.)
But this is not possible.

Under the buried
church tower
tolls the bell.
Centuries of rubble
echo in its sound.

2.

Silence
is a lonely refuge.
It is my favorite music.
It flickers in harmony
with the black and white
bird, the one that refuses
to leave us,
the small body that darts ahead,
into the bushes, the branches speechless,
as we approach.

3.

There isn't much to say, really,
but sadness teaches.
Mourning is a thread of common life.
My father, for instance, his cheek-skin
sags and the war scars
seem to widen as he sleeps.
A darkness so deep, he totters
at the precipice.

For years as a child, I prayed
(with great longing)
to fall in. There to be greeted
by the wounded and dead
as a long lost son.

The battle still rages overhead.

4.

The beautiful colors portray a world
almost perfect. They spark and flicker
from the tenement's highest windows.
But within my television, you can see
only the sickly green that rolls,
so smoothly, into a dead sea
of plastic. Its weight increases
as the stillness rises, volcanic,
almost perfect.

5.

The path through the woods is long,
the way predictably dark. And yet,
each and every tree can be transformed
into a Cross
if we could only find the interest.
And the right start.

The narrow suckers
shoot upward from every tree.
You must cut them off if you want the tree to grow.
But in what direction, and what for—
the centuries are so few.
Not upward into nothing. To save us each
from darkness, there is a single
thorn of light.
There is nothing but a sense of panic in the endless space.

6.

The soul
is a seed, they say,
floating
slowly
homeward
toward eternity.

7.
This is what they say.
I do not believe them,
and yet . . .

vaporized, we survive
as shadows
on masonry walls,

even when the buildings
are no more. Torn down.
blasted away.

Centuries
of rubble
buried beneath the earth.

8.
My feet slide loosely in my ill-fitted shoes.
In each, there is a shard,
a new beginning, a small mirror
of flesh and blood. Confine us right
and we will grow; wrong
and the future holds dominion over all the trees.

I am happiest with nothing
vibrating toward me through the open air.
The combat helicopter overhead

is in training. The total disruption blasts away
the rock-
hard self. As does silence.
The injury is internal.

9.
Thin black streams
of smoke
rise and swirl
through the branches
mixing with loud
bursts
of white steam.

The burning buildings,
the encroaching city.

As the columns reach the sky,
they seem to panic
and then disperse,
like distressed spirits drowning
into an ocean of light.

10.
But the wind
never leaves us.
It brings the past,

the errors of ancient cities,
armies dead and buried,
tyrants, victims, lovers, martyrs,
the lost robe of Christ ... dust.

Matter that cannot be
created or destroyed,
was destroyed and reborn
as the shadowed future
into which I walk, ash that I breath.

Minuscule seeds that settle, seemingly forever,
deeper and deeper,
into the dark.

                11.
Cowering in city basements,
shivering within the strong arms
of fear—oh crumbling cement,
oh dampness, the sickness,
be thankful for the darkness. And the sun,
broken by the branches,
lights up the path so delicately,
you look down through the stained
windows of a church
and step on the fallen, in silence,

the silence which is broken.

Hearing Them

Some of those saints were a long time ago.
I didn't want the sourceless suffering to interfere;
not this time, not when the unidentifiable
music had entered through the skylight, a woman's soul,
brunette or blond, cascading through the glass,
against the coming of the light, a life we had never wanted,
against the smart of a door
slammed against the face, the broken
nose and cheekbone, the beautiful colors and rage.
Some of those saints were a long time ago,
a long time coming, with a long heroic past,
and a hope. And some with their faith,
and their father, and the wind
which wrapped the trunk
of a large, weathered oak
before it let loose, rose, tying the spirit on its sound,
this sound, on a warm winter's night.
I didn't want to interfere; I had to hope.
Some of those saints, I knew, were certainly
a long time ago. But their spirits rose
and fell into my ears, down through my ears,
right through the sky, through the bandages and glass.

ACKNOWLEDGMENTS

Epigraph to "Architectural Digest" from *The Poetry of Robert Frost* edited by Edward Connery Lathem. Copyright © 1951 by Robert Frost. Copyright 1923, © 1969 by Henry Holt & Co. Reprinted by permission of Henry Holt & Co. Inc.

Epigraph to "The Hieratic Head of Pound" from *Ezra Pound: The Cantos of Ezra Pound.* Copyright © 1948 by Ezra Pound. Reprinted by permission of New Directions Publishing Corp.

Last line of "New Moon" and brief paraphrases in "Loss" from *Collected Poems 1909–1962* by T.S. Eliot, copyright © 1936 by Harcourt Brace Jovanovich Inc; copyright © 1963, 1964 by T.S. Eliot.

Epigraph to "The God of Fish" from *Selected Poems* by Robert Bly, copyright © 1986 by Robert Bly. Reprinted by permission of HarperCollins Publishers.

Lines 157 and 158 of "Loss" ("removed from the vibration of air, they lived through the eyes") from *New Selected Poems* by Ted Hughes, copyright © 1982 by Ted Hughes. Reprinted by permission of HarperCollins Publishers, and Faber & Faber LTD.

Italicized words on pages 52 and 63 from John Berryman. Reprinted by permission of Farrar, Straus and Giroux, Inc.: Excerpt from "The Ball Poem" from *Collected Poems: 1937–1971* by John Berryman. Copyright © 1989 by Kate Donahue Berryman. Excerpt from "Many's the dawn" from *The Dream Songs* by John Berryman. Copyright © 1969 by John Berryman.

Last sentence of section #24 of "Loss" from *Dante's Inferno,* translated by Mark Musa, copyright © 1971 by Indiana University Press. Reprinted by permission of Indiana University Press.